Illustrated by
Sarah Long

# CATRIONA CLARKE

# SHE SHOOTS, SHE SCORES!

KINGFISHER

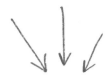

For Caro – C.C.
For my dad. Thumbs up – S.L.

A Raspberry Book
www.raspberrybooks.co.uk
Written by Catriona Clarke
Illustrated by Sarah Long
Editorial: Tracey Turner
Art direction & cover design:
Sidonie Beresford-Browne
Design: Sophie Willcox

KINGFISHER

First published 2021 by Kingfisher
an imprint of Macmillan Children's Books
a division of Pan Macmillan
The Smithson, 6 Briset Street, London, EC1M 5NR
Associated companies throughout the world
www.panmacmillan.com

EU representative: Macmillan Publishers Ireland Ltd, 1st Floor,
The Liffey Trust Centre, 117-126 Sheriff Street Upper, Dublin 1, D01 YC43

ISBN 978-0-7534-4628-7

Printed in China
4 6 8 9 7 5 3
3TR/0623/RV/WKT/140MA

MIX
Paper | Supporting
responsible forestry
FSC® C116313
FSC
www.fsc.org

# CONTENTS

# FOREWORD BY STEPH HOUGHTON

I hope you enjoy reading this book about my favourite subject – football!

When I was growing up, my family supported my love for the game. My football heroes were English players David Beckham and Kevin Phillips, who inspired me to want to play. I always followed my team – Sunderland, the club Kevin Phillips played for. One day I wanted to be able to wear that red and white shirt. And one day, I did!

In any career there are challenges to overcome. One of mine was that women's football wasn't taken seriously, and women and girls weren't encouraged to play. When I was young, female football wasn't that popular, and I'm glad to have seen how that's changed. I also suffered injuries which meant I had to miss two major tournaments for my country.

However, I feel that setbacks and challenges have made me the person I am today. They may have knocked me down, but I came back stronger and more determined to be the best I can be. As a result, I've been able to experience some amazing memories with clubs like Arsenal and my current club, Manchester City. Being able to lead these teams and lift major trophies makes the sacrifices and hard work worthwhile.

I'm very proud that I was able to captain and play for my country over a hundred times. Some of my favourite memories are winning bronze at the 2015 FIFA Women's World Cup, and being a part of the Team GB Olympic team in 2012 in London.

I hope this book inspires you to play, watch and support this fantastic sport!

Steph Houghton

# THE BEAUTIFUL GAME

THERE'S NOTHING QUITE LIKE FOOTBALL . . .

The amazing team spirit.

The nail-biting tension of a penalty shootout.

THE ROAR OF THE CROWD.

**And the utter JOY when your team wins!**

I think football is the *best game in the world,* and women's football is <u>particularly brilliant.</u> More than **30 million girls and women** play football around the world – it's the most popular women's team sport by a long way. *And it's getting more and more popular every day.*

The 2019 FIFA Women's World Cup smashed TV viewing records. The final between the USA and the Netherlands was the most watched women's football match of all time, with an incredible **263 million viewers** around the world. Were you one of them? *I was!*

In total, **1.12 billion people** watched some of the World Cup in 2019. *Pretty amazing, right?*

But things haven't always looked so rosy for women's football. There have been <u>dramas and difficulties</u> on the long journey to get us where we are today. *Read on to find out the highs and lows of the women's beautiful game . . .*

# A BOLD BEGINNING

In the 1890s, things weren't so great for women. They didn't have the same rights as men, and men thought they were better at everything. Women were supposed to be dignified. They weren't supposed to run around a football field getting muddy . . . but that's exactly what a group of British women wanted to do. This was the start of the women's game.

Nettie and the North London team. She's second from the left on the back row.

## Nettie Honeyball

As well as having the BEST NAME EVER, Nettie Honeyball formed the first British Ladies' Football Club in 1895.

### The British Ladies' Football Club

**L**adies' Football Match, North v. South, wil be played on the Maidenhead Football Ground on Easter Monday Afternoon. Kick-Off at 3.30 pm. Admission 6d.

*Enclosure & Pavilion 1s. extra. Ladies desirous of joining the above Club should apply to Miss Nettie J. Honeyball, "Ellesmere", 27, Weston Park, Crouch End, N.*

The very first match was advertised in English newspapers.

Nettie said,

*"There is no reason why football should not be played by women, and played well, too."*

Quite right, Nettie!

Around 10,000 people came to watch Nettie's match. Some of the spectators cheered, but others shouted horrible things. Newspaper articles about the match mocked the women players, often commenting on how they looked. But this just made Nettie even more determined. She took women's football teams on a tour of England.

# Wartime Workers

Strangely, the outbreak of World War I in 1914 helped women's football. Men's teams were disbanded, and women took over the men's jobs in the factories. Factory owners thought that it might be good for the workers to play football. They weren't doing it to be nice – they thought it would make the women work harder!

# Dick, Kerr

Lily Parr was the star player of a famous factory team called Dick, Kerr Ladies. She was only 14 when she joined. She was strong, fast and had excellent ball control. She went on to score more than 900 goals.

*Lily Parr*

## FOOTIE FACT

A match in 1920 between Dick, Kerr Ladies and St Helens Ladies was attended by 53,000 people – that's about the same as an English Premier League match today! There were another 14,000 disappointed fans left outside the ground.

By 1920, Dick, Kerr Ladies was one of around 150 English women's football teams. But things were about to *go very, very wrong* . . .

# BANNED AND BACK AGAIN

Women's football became more and more popular all over the world, and especially in the UK. But some people weren't too happy about the success of the women's game.

## The Boys Are Back

The Football Association (FA) in England had been happy for enormous crowds to watch women's matches during World War I, but now the men were back and men's teams were playing again. What if people actually preferred watching the women's games? Something had to be done!

On 5 December 1921, the FA passed a ban on women's football. Women were no longer allowed to play on men's grounds. The reason? Apparently the FA had consulted with medical experts and decided that:

## Around the World

Lots of countries followed suit. France banned the women's game in 1932. Brazil banned it in 1941. West Germany (Germany was divided into East and West back then) passed their ban in 1955. Their football association said:

*"This aggressive sport is essentially alien to the nature of woman ... The display of the woman's body offends decency and modesty."*

*"Football is quite unsuitable for females."*

WHAT A LOAD OF NONSENSE!

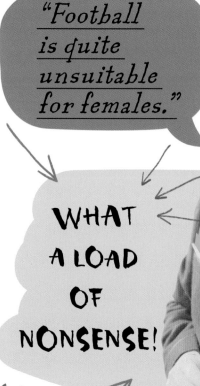

This epic display of stupidity didn't stop women from playing football, it just made things a lot harder.

Preston Ladies Football Club playing against a Belgian team in 1939. It looks like they enjoyed themselves, too.

# MANCHESTER CORINTHIANS

Manchester Corinthians

In 1949, a man called Percy Ashley from Manchester, England, was disappointed that he couldn't find a team for his daughter, Doris, to play on. Doris *loved* football. So Percy set up a team himself!

The Manchester Corinthians ranged from 13 to 40 years old and trained at a park every Sunday. They changed in a hut and there was no running water for a wash after training – they had to carry buckets of water.

The Corinthians went on to huge success, touring Europe, South America and North Africa, often playing matches to raise money for charity. In 1959, they won an unofficial European Cup. All this, despite not being able to play on proper football grounds back home.

**Seeing Sense**

In 1971 – after a full 50 YEARS – the FA ban on women playing on men's club grounds was finally lifted. Bans in other countries, including West Germany, Brazil and France, were eventually lifted too. But the bans did A LOT of damage to women's football and it's still struggling to catch up – all because of terrible decisions made by men.

Yay!

# INSPIRING STORIES

## TEENAGE DREAM

The 1971 England team.

In the summer of 1971, an unofficial Women's World Cup took place in Mexico. The tournament included teams from France, Argentina, Denmark, Italy, Mexico and England – even though very few people followed women's football in the UK.

## Caleb & Co

The English team was very young. At 13, midfielder Leah Caleb was the youngest player, but several were teenagers, and som were still at school. Leah Caleb was often compared to George Best, one of the best male players in the world.

### Leah Caleb

## A Warm Welcome

Mexico was football-crazy – they didn't mind if men or women were playing. The England players were amazed to find a huge crowd of fans to greet them at the airport. They were asked for autographs and invited to parties. They even appeared on TV – this was NOTHING like back home!

AERONAVES DE MEXICO

AERONAVES DE MEXICO

# The Tournament

The tournament was a massive success. Ninety thousand people attended the match between England and Mexico, which Mexico won 4-0. England didn't win any of their matches, but just taking part was a dream come true.

England winger Gill Sayell was 14 years old at the time. Later, she said:

"FOR A SCHOOLGIRL, TO BE PLUCKED INTO THAT LIMELIGHT WAS QUITE SURREAL."

# Back to Reality

After the tournament, the British newspapers mostly ignored the England team and the tournament. When Leah Caleb returned to school, the head teacher didn't even bother to mention it in assembly!

But it wasn't all bad news. The young team of 1971 blazed a trail for women and girls in the future. It took another 20 years before there was an official Women's World Cup, but they had kicked things off.

Mexico lost 3-0 to Denmark in the final. All three Danish goals were scored by another teenager, 15-year-old Susanne Augustesen. Around 110,000 spectators watched the final, but the figure is not official, so it's not in any of the history books.

# FOOTIE FACT

Before the tournament, there were reports of pink and white goalposts and beauty salons in the changing rooms! Thankfully, that didn't really happen.

# INSPIRING STORIES

## ROSE REILLY

Rose Reilly was born in Stewarton, Scotland in 1955. She was obsessed with football from the age of four, but no one could ever have predicted where that obsession would take her!

## Rose in Disguise

Rose started playing for a local boys' club when she was seven, but the coach insisted that she get her hair cut and call herself Ross so that no one would realize she was a girl. Rose didn't mind – she would do whatever it took to be able to play. Her mum wasn't so happy when she saw the haircut, though!

A scout from top team Celtic watched Rose score seven goals in one match. He wanted to sign "the boy who got all the goals", but because Rose was a girl, he couldn't! Rose thought she was good enough to sign with Celtic, and she was probably right.

Rose joined an adult women's team when she was just 12. She took on part-time jobs like delivering newspapers so she could buy her football kit.

## Italian Star

Rose was desperate to play football professionally. She couldn't do that in Scotland, because the Scottish Football Association still didn't support the women's game. She moved to France and then Italy, where she played for AC Milan, and matches attracted thousands of fans.

# Top Scot

In 1984, Italy hosted an unofficial Women's World Cup called the Mundialito Femminile. The Italian president asked Rose to play for the Italian national team, even though she was Scottish. Of course, she said yes! Italy went on to win the tournament, and Rose scored a goal in their 3-1 win over West Germany in the final. To this day, Rose Reilly is the only Scottish player to lift a World Cup.

## FOOTIE FACT

For one season, Rose managed to play for both AC Milan in Italy AND Reims in France. She travelled between the two countries with two kits in her luggage. Both teams won their leagues that season!

Rose Reilly went on to play for nine Italian clubs over 20 years, winning loads of championships and trophies. She is undoubtedly the most successful Scottish footballer of all time, and everybody should know her name.

# THE WOMEN'S WORLD CUP

## Fearful FIFA

The first official FIFA Women's World Cup was hosted by China in 1991. That's 61 years after the first men's World Cup!

FIFA (the organization in charge of world football) was worried the first tournament would be a flop and hurt the reputation of the men's World Cup. So they hid the all-important "World Cup" bit. The full name was "The FIFA World Championship for Women's Football for the M&M's World Cup", which is a bit of a mouthful!

The tournament turned out to be a massive success.

The USA were the winners, beating Norway in the final. But when the USA team returned home, hardly anyone seemed to care. That would all change over the coming years.

## FOOTIE FACT

The World Cup matches were only 80 minutes long, because the organizers felt that women would find the full 90 minutes too tiring. FIFA even considered making the players use smaller footballs. <u>Thank goodness they had second thoughts about that idea.</u>

# Progress

The 1995 tournament was held in Sweden. The tournament was now simply called the FIFA Women's World Cup and the games were a full 90 minutes. This time the organizers allowed teams a two-minute 'time-out' in each half – annoyingly, they still thought that women couldn't quite manage a match of football as well as the men.

This tournament saw the official World Cup debuts of Australia, Canada and England. In the final, Norway scored two goals in the space of three minutes in the first half, and went on to beat Germany 2-0. One in four Norwegians watched the victory on TV!

# A Turning Point

The 1999 Women's World Cup was held in the USA. The home team bus got stuck in traffic on the way to the first game, and the players were stunned to realize that they were the cause of the traffic jam – tens of thousands of people were headed to watch their match. It was the first sign that this tournament would be a real game-changer.

The final was decided with a nail-biting penalty shootout, ending in a win for the home team and one of the most famous sporting photos of all time. Brandi Chastain was so excited after scoring the winning penalty that she whipped off her jersey.

The 1999 Women's World Cup blew away any doubts about the women's game. The players paved the way for all who followed. Girls all over the world were inspired by what they saw, and women's football was now officially

## A BIG DEAL.

# WORLD CUP STATS AND FACTS

Since 1991, the Women's World Cup has wowed us with outstanding goals, nail-biting matches, unforgettable moments, and LOTS of surprises along the way.

In 2015 Carli Lloyd became the first woman to record a hat-trick (three goals) in a World Cup final – against Japan in just 16 minutes!

The 2015 tournament in Canada was played on artificial grass. The players were NOT happy about it. It makes injuries more likely and gets very hot. Fingers crossed all World Cups stick to real grass in the future.

An outbreak of the SARS virus meant that the World Cup in 2003 had to be played in the USA again instead of China as planned. But China got to host in 2007.

The USA beat Thailand 13-0 in the 2019 Women's World Cup. Not surprisingly, it was the biggest win in any World Cup.

In a 1995 World Cup match against Denmark, US forward Mia Hamm played in goal for the last few minutes after the goalie was sent off. She made two saves and the USA won 2-0!

The youngest ever Women's World Cup player was Ifeanyi Chiejine of Nigeria. She was just 16 years and one month old when she played for her country in 1999.

Australian Ellyse Perry played in both the women's cricket World Cup in 2009 AND the women's football World Cup in 2011.

# FORMIGA

Brazilian player Formiga (Portuguese for "Ant") became the oldest ever Women's World Cup player at the 2019 tournament. She was 41 years (and 98 days!) old.

Formiga is also the first player to appear at SEVEN World Cups. What an achievement!

| YEAR | HOST NATION | FINAL (winner in bold) | SCORE |
|------|-------------|------------------------|-------|
| 1991 | China | **USA** v Norway | 2-1 |
| 1995 | Sweden | **Norway** v Sweden | 2-0 |
| 1999 | USA | **USA** v China | 0-0 then 5-4 on penalties |
| 2003 | USA | **Germany** v Sweden | 2-1 in extra time |
| 2007 | China | **Germany** v Brazil | 2-0 |
| 2011 | Germany | **Japan** v USA | 2-2 then 3-1 on penalties |
| 2015 | Canada | **USA** v Japan | 5-2 |
| 2019 | France | **USA** v Netherlands | 2-0 |

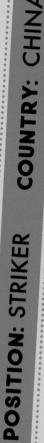

**COUNTRY: CHINA**

**POSITION: STRIKER**

# SUN WEN

## EARLY YEARS:

Wen started playing football aged ten, encouraged by her dad. At her local sports school, when she was 17, her coach told her she should give up playing because she wasn't very good. Luckily, Wen didn't believe him! She moved to another team and worked even harder. Less than a year later, she was selected for the Chinese national team.

## ACHIEVEMENTS:

★ Played in four Women's World Cups.

★ In the 1999 World Cup, she won both the Golden Boot for top scorer and Golden Ball for top player.

★ With Michelle Akers, named FIFA's Female Player of the Century in 2000.

★ Retired in 2006 and is considered one of the all-time greats of the women's game.

# MICHELLE AKERS

POSITION: STRIKER / MIDFIELDER  COUNTRY: USA

## EARLY YEARS:

Michelle dreamed of playing American football, but girls weren't allowed, so she tried football ("soccer" in the USA) instead. It turned out she was very good at it! She kept playing, though she sometimes had to tape up her football boots when her family couldn't afford to buy a new pair.

## ACHIEVEMENTS:

★ Played in the first US women's team in 1985, and was the first player to score a goal.

★ With Sun Wen, named FIFA's Female Player of the Century in 2000.

★ Led the USA to victory in the first official Women's World Cup in 1991, scoring ten goals.

★ Retired in 2000 after scoring 105 goals in 153 international matches. She was the USA's first great star, and one of the greatest of all time.

# KITTED OUT

The clothes women have worn to play football have changed A LOT since Nettie Honeyball's day . . .

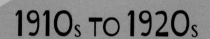

## 1910s TO 1920s

The hats were to keep hair from getting muddy, but they probably just got sweaty instead. The shorts were a bit more practical than before.

## 1890s

You'd work up quite a sweat running around in this lot. Nettie Honeyball was one of the first women's players to wear long shorts instead of a skirt. People disapproved, but she didn't care.

# 1970s to 1990s

Women mostly wore men's kits. They were baggy and didn't fit very well.

# 2020s

Shirts are now closely fitted, but not as tight as men's shirts. Finally, football kits are especially made to fit women's bodies, and, for the first time ever, players are actually asked about their kit. How on earth did it take this long?

# INSPIRING STORIES

## FINDING HOPE

The 2011 Women's World Cup was held in Germany, and most people expected Germany or the USA to win it. But that's not what happened. This is the story of a group of women inspired to greatness by something bigger than football.

## Disaster Strikes

On 11 March 2011, a massive earthquake hit northeastern Japan. The earthquake caused a tsunami, which destroyed thousands of buildings and caused a meltdown at the Fukushima nuclear power plant. Nearly 16,000 people died, and millions were left without power. It was one of the worst natural disasters in the country's history.

The Japanese women's team weren't sure if they should take part in a World Cup at such a difficult time. Surely there were more important things to worry about? But in the end, they decided to play in the tournament, hoping to encourage and uplift people back home.

## The Road to the Final

Japan had a tricky first round. But in the knockout stages, the team started to shine. They'd never before got this far in a World Cup. Before the quarter-final match against Germany, the team watched a film of the disaster back home to remind them of what they were playing for. They went on to win 1-0 in extra time. In the semi-final, Japan beat Sweden 3-1. They were through to the final . . . could they possibly go all the way?

## The Final

The stronger, taller USA team dominated the final from the start, but Japan didn't give up. The captain, Homare Sawa, said, "We ran and ran – we were exhausted but we kept running." They forced the game into extra time, but all seemed lost when Abby Wambach scored in the 104th minute. The score was now 2-1, and time was running out . . .

But Japan won a corner with just four minutes to play, and Homare Sawa scored a miracle goal. Facing away from the goal, she somehow managed to flick the ball past all the players in the box, and past the world's best goalkeeper, Hope Solo.

Sawa says it's the best goal she's ever scored.

HOMARE SAWA'S AMAZING GOAL

After extra time, the score was 2-2. A penalty shootout would decide the match. To everyone's surprise, Team USA faltered in the shootout, and a brilliant strike by Saki Kumagai sealed the victory for Japan.

Japan!

Yay! Japan!

Through teamwork, determination and hard work, Japan had won the World Cup. It was wonderful for them, and it gave people watching back home something to celebrate after months of hardship and sadness. On the pitch, the team unfurled a banner with a message to the rest of the world.

# OLYMPIQUE LYONNAIS

France is home to the best football team in the world. They hardly EVER lose. They are Olympique Lyonnais Féminin, and the team is so good that it's hard to think of a team in ANY sport that comes even close to their success.

## A Bold Vision

Jean-Michel Aulas, the president of the men's football club Olympique Lyonnais, decided to launch a women's team. Plenty of top clubs in Europe already had women's teams, but Jean-Michel did things differently, treating the men's and women's teams exactly the same. They have the same training facilities, and the players often socialize together.

Jean-Michel was also willing to spend A LOT of money. Top male footballers earn millions and millions of pounds. Top female footballers earn nowhere near that much, but Olympique Lyonnais Féminin pay their players better than any other women's team in the world.

# Star Players

The team attracts the world's best players. And having the best players brings more great players to the team – footballers want to play with the best, so that they can improve their own game. That's why top US stars Megan Rapinoe (below), Catarina Macario and Alex Morgan have all played for Olympique Lyonnais Féminin, and most of the French national side play for them too.

## FOOTIE FACT

Olympique Lyonnais first contacted Megan Rapinoe on Facebook to see if she was interested in playing for the club – she most definitely was!

## The Academy

Around 400 talented girls and boys attend the Olympique Lyonnais youth academy. They live, train and study together. As well as providing top-class football training and schooling, the club looks after the players' mental wellbeing. Breathing exercises and yoga are part of their daily routine. It must work, because about one third of the current Olympique Lyonnais Féminin team came through the youth academy!

POSITION: RIGHT-BACK    COUNTRY: ENGLAND

# LUCY BRONZE

**FOOTIE FACT**

Lucy overcame many injuries early in her career. Maybe it's no coincidence that her middle name is Tough!

## EARLY YEARS:

Lucy was the only girl on her school's football team. When she was 11, she had to leave, because the English Football Association thought that girls would get hurt if they played alongside boys after the age of 12. But this didn't put Lucy off – she just had to travel much further from home to play.

## ACHIEVEMENTS:

★ The first defender – and the first English player – to be named UEFA's Women's Footballer of the Year in 2019.

★ Widely regarded as the world's best right back.

★ Awarded the Silver Ball in the 2019 Women's World Cup and was named the Best FIFA Women's Player in 2020.

★ Played all six games of England's triumphant EURO 2022 campaign.

# WENDIE RENARD

POSITION: CENTRE-BACK

## FOOTIE FACT

At 187cm, Wendie was the tallest player in the 2019 Women's World Cup.

## EARLY YEARS:

When she was seven years old, Wendie watched the French women's team on TV. She told her mum that one day she would play for France. Her mum laughed . . . but Wendie went ahead and did it!

## ACHIEVEMENTS:

★ She has scored more than 100 goals for Olympique Lyonnais and more than 30 for France – not bad for a defender! Her height and ability in the air means Wendie is always a goal threat.

★ Joined Olympique Lyonnais in 2006 and is currently the captain.

# INSPIRING STORIES

## ASISAT OSHOALA

Asisat Oshoala is a brilliant attacking midfielder and forward who made the tough choice to defy her parents and follow her dream. Now she's an inspiration to young footballers everywhere.

## Growing up

Asisat was born in Lagos, Nigeria. She fell in love with football at a young age, but her mum wasn't pleased. She wouldn't give Asisat money for food if she caught her playing football on the streets with the boys!

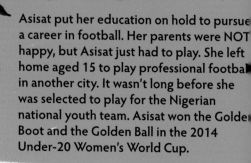

Asisat put her education on hold to pursue a career in football. Her parents were NOT happy, but Asisat just had to play. She left home aged 15 to play professional football in another city. It wasn't long before she was selected to play for the Nigerian national youth team. Asisat won the Golden Boot and the Golden Ball in the 2014 Under-20 Women's World Cup.

## Around the World

Asisat Oshoala made headlines as the first African footballer to play in the English Women's Super League when she signed with Liverpool in 2015. Sadly, she was injured and had to sit out some of the season. But things looked up when she joined Arsenal – and won the Women's FA Cup in 2016.

Next, Asisat went to China, where she played for Dalian Quanjian. She thrived in China's Super League, and her team won both the league and cup titles. She was named the best player in the league in 2017. In 2019, Asisat signed with Barcelona Femení – the best team in Spain.

# Super Falcons

Asisat Oshoala is one of the stars of the Nigerian national team, nicknamed the Super Falcons. They are the most successful African national team by a long way – they've qualified for every World Cup so far. In 2019, Asisat helped them reach the last 16 of the World Cup in France. She scored one of the best goals of the tournament against South Korea in the group stage.

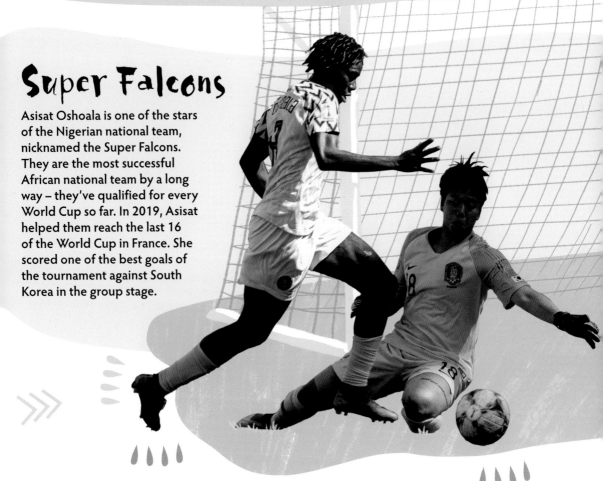

# Giving Back

Asisat is a huge star in Nigeria, and she's helping more young girls to get involved in her sport. The Asisat Oshoala Youth Foundation gives opportunities to the next generation of players. Part of its job is to educate parents, showing them that girls can and should play football, and that they can play the game and get a good education at the same time.

Asisat Oshoala is a role model to young girls in Nigeria and all over the world.

# GREAT GOALKEEPING

The goalkeeper's position can be the loneliest on the pitch. There are long stretches of doing nothing at all, then sudden frantic action when the other team attacks. Goalies are under a lot of pressure. Goalkeeping is not for wimps!

**So, what are the qualities that make a great goalkeeper?**

### CONCENTRATION
You have to stay alert at all times.

### RESILIENCE
If you make a mistake, you have to bounce back quickly.

### COURAGE
It takes a lot of bravery to put your body on the line and do whatever it takes to stop a goal.

### REFLEXES
Must be lightning fast to react to shots on goal.

### LEADERSHIP
As goalie, you're in the perfect position to organize the defence and inspire the whole team to victory.

The USA's Hope Solo is probably the greatest women's goalkeeper of all time. She said:

"A great goal keeper canno win a game. She can only save it."

## HOW TO SAVE A PENALTY

**1.** Watch the penalty taker's eyes. She will often kick the ball to the corner opposite to where she's looking.

**2.** Stand your ground until the very last second. Don't dive too early!

**3.** Remember that most right-footed players kick the ball to the goalkeeper's right, and most left-footed players go for the goalkeeper's left.

**4.** Don't forget that saving a penalty is HARD. If you manage it, you'll be a hero!

## FOOTIE FACT

Christiane Endler is one of the best young goalkeepers in the world. She was awarded Player of the Match for Chile against the USA in the 2019 World Cup after making several spectacular saves – even though her team lost 3-0.

## SCORE   3 : 0   SCORE

# SARI VAN VEENENDAAL

**POSITION: GOALKEEPER COUNTRY: NETHERLANDS**

## EARLY YEARS:

Sari tried lots of different sports as a child – badminton, swimming, volleyball, basketball and athletics. But when she discovered football at 12 years old, she knew she'd found her passion.

## ACHIEVEMENTS:

In UEFA Women's EURO 2017, she started in all six matches, and conceded just three goals. The Dutch team went on to win the tournament.

Captain of the Dutch team until she retired in 2022.

★ Won the Golden Glove (best goalkeeper) at the 2019 World Cup in France and was voted best female goalkeeper in the world by FIFA in the same year.

★ Made EIGHT saves in the final of the 2019 World Cup against USA.

# DEFEND!

Defenders don't always get the credit they deserve. They are football's unsung heroes, swooping in to save the day.

Great defenders often share the same qualities. How many boxes would you tick? Maybe you would make a great defender too!

 **CALM UNDER PRESSURE**
If you panic, you make mistakes. And a mistake can mean the other team scores a goal.

 **CONFIDENT**
You have to be confident when making a tackle.

 **SELFLESS**
You have to be willing to put your body on the line to stop the other team.

 **DISCIPLINED**
If you commit a foul, it gives the other team a GREAT chance to score a goal. Make sure you play by the rules!

 **STRONG**
Don't let yourself get pushed around by the other team.

Tackling is a crucial skill for all footballers but especially for defenders.

## TACKLING TIPS

1. Never tackle from behind or with your studs up – it's dangerous!

2. Decide if you NEED to make the tackle. Maybe it would be better to let the opposing player keep the ball for now, as long as you keep them away from the goal.

3. Decide if the ball is close enough for you to win.

4. Check the position of your teammates – the tackle might be too risky if you don't make it.

5. Stay on your feet, so you can recover quickly if you don't make the tackle.

6. Be confident with your tackle and time it perfectly.

New Zealand's Abby Erceg is one of the best in the business.

# BECKY SAUERBRUNN

**COUNTRY: USA**

**POSITION: CENTRE-BACK**

"Whoever wants the ball more is going to win it."

## EARLY YEARS:

When she was 14, Becky watched a match between USA and Nigeria at the 1999 World Cup. Carly Overbeck was the captain of the US team that went on to win the tournament. Becky modelled her playing style on Carly's: she wanted to be as efficient, smart and competitive as her hero.

## ACHIEVEMENTS:

Has been named Defender of the Year in the National Women's Soccer League a record FOUR times.

Loves reading almost as much as she loves football (especially science fiction and fantasy)!

★ After she was dropped from the Under-23 US Women's team for not being fast enough, she started working extra hard to be smarter. Now she is often described as "the smartest player on the field," because she uses her brain as much as her pace, skill and strength.

# MIDFIELD

Midfield is the engine of the team, driving it forward. Acting as the link between the defenders and the forwards, midfielders have a lot of work to do.

In a match, the midfielders usually run the furthest, have the most touches on the ball, and make the most passes. A strong midfield is vital to any team.

There are different roles in midfield – defensive, attacking, central, wide – but all the best midfielders need to be . . .

### EXTREMELY FIT
*You are always moving in midfield.*

### HARD-WORKING
*You can't afford to stop concentrating for a second.*

### COMPOSED
*Keeping calm is vital for decision making.*

### QUICK-THINKING
*You need to react quickly to other players' moves.*

### DECISIVE
*Make a decision and stick to it!*

### SKILLED
*A good midfielder has a wide range of skills.*

## WHAT DOES A MIDFIELDER HAVE TO DO?

1. Provide smooth and efficient transitions between defence and attack.

2. Keep the ball! Maintaining possession is crucial to stop the other team from scoring.

3. Set the pace of play, speeding up and slowing down as necessary.

4. Stop attacks from the other team – midfield is the first line of defence.

5. Assist and score goals. Midfielders often take free kicks and long shots outside the box. Sometimes a midfielder takes on the other team's defence all by herself.

Norway's Caroline Graham Hansen is one of the most creative midfielders in the game. She also scores LOADS of goals.

# SAKI KUMAGAI

**POSITION: DEFENSIVE MIDFIELDER  COUNTRY: JAPAN**

"If football didn't exist, I couldn't express myself – it's my life. Without football, life is less interesting and too serious. You always have to laugh."

## EARLY YEARS:

There were no girls' teams in the town where Saki grew up, so she played football with boys until she was 15 years old. She debuted for the national team when she was just 17!

## ACHIEVEMENTS:

Also known for scoring important penalties – scored the winning penalty for Olympique Lyonnais in the UEFA Women's Champions League final in 2016.

Captain of Japan's national team.

★ Named Asian Football Confederation's Women's Player of the Year 2019.

★ One of the most talented defensive midfielders in the game – she rarely gives the ball away, and she's already thinking about her next move, even before she's got the ball.

# UP FRONT

Football is about scoring goals, and it's the forwards' job to score them. Forwards get the most attention – they're often the game's biggest stars – but they're also under a lot of pressure.

## TOP GOAL-SCORING TIPS

1. KEEP MOVING – never stand still while waiting for the ball.

2. Know what you're going to do before you receive the ball.

3. Be decisive – don't overthink things.

4. Check the position of the goalkeeper before you shoot.

5. Learn to shoot with both feet.

If you want to be a forward, you need to have . . .

### SHOOTING SKILLS
*You have to be able to get the ball in the back of the net (as often as possible!).*

### CALMNESS AND CONCENTRATION
*You can't afford to stop concentrating for a second.*

### STRENGTH
*You can't let yourself get pushed around by defenders.*

### SPEED
*Your speed will help you put the defence under pressure. You can dribble the ball past defenders, or make runs into space so your teammates can pass you the ball.*

Vivianne Miedema of the Netherlands is one of the world's best forwards. She's known for her poise, positioning and excellent shooting ability.

## FOOTIE FACT

In 2020, Christine Sinclair overtook the USA's Abby Wambach to become the world's top international goalscorer. By 2023, she had scored an incredible 190 goals for Canada.

# SAM KERR

"The team is always most important. Without your team, you can't achieve anything."

## EARLY YEARS:

Sam hated football when she was little, and only started playing when she was 12. Three years later, she played her first match for the Australian national team at just 15 years old!

## ACHIEVEMENTS:

★ Captain of the Australian team, known for her speed, skill and back-flip goal celebrations!

★ Suffered a career-threatening foot injury in 2015, but came back stronger than ever.

★ In 2019, she became the first Australian player – male or female – to score a hat-trick in a World Cup.

★ All-time leading scorer in the US National Women's Soccer League AND second-highest scorer in Australia's A-League Women.

# GOING FOR GOLD

The Olympic Games are the pinnacle of sporting achievement. The Games are held every four years, with more than 200 countries coming together to compete against each other in more than 30 different sports.

Women's football was first included in the Olympics in 1996, when the home team, the USA, beat China to the gold medal.

## Top Scorer

When she was little, Brazil's Cristiane chopped the heads off her dolls so she could play football with them. The sacrifice of those poor dolls was worth it, because Cristiane grew up to be a football superstar.

CRISTIANE

No player – male or female – has scored more Olympic goals than Cristiane. She's scored 14 goals over four Olympic Games, helping Brazil to win silver medals in Athens (2004) and Beijing (2008).

## FOOTIE FACT

Norway beat USA to the gold medal at the Sydney 2000 Olympics with a golden goal. The golden goal rule means that the first team to score a goal in extra time wins the match – there's no chance for the other team to equalize.

# Teamwork Makes the Dream Work

Germany had won the bronze medal three times, in 2000, 2004 and 2008. In Rio in 2016, they were desperate for gold. They faced Sweden in the final, in front of a crowd of more than 50,000 fans.

Germany's Dzsenifer Marozsan scored the first goal just after half time, then disaster struck

for Sweden with an own goal by defender Linda Sembrant. Sweden's Stina Blackstenius managed to score, but it was too late. Germany won the match 2-1. They were finally Olympic champions.

Germany's defensive midfielder, Melanie Behringer, described the reason for her team's triumph at the Rio Olympics:

"Our team spirit was our secret weapon because we didn't play the best football, but our togetherness couldn't be beaten."

Teamwork is vital in football. Individual stars are important, but teams can only achieve great things if players truly work together and support each other.

| ⬤⬤⬤⬤⬤ | 🥇 | 🥈 | 🥉 |
|---|---|---|---|
| 1996 Atlanta, USA | USA | China | Norway |
| 2000 Sydney, Australia | Norway | USA | Germany |
| 2004 Athens, Greece | USA | Brazil | Germany |
| 2008 Beijing, China | USA | Brazil | Germany |
| 2012 London, UK | USA | Japan | Canada |
| 2016 Rio de Janeiro, Brazil | Germany | Sweden | Canada |
| 2021 Tokyo, Japan | Canada | Sweden | USA |

# SIMPLY THE BEST

The US women's football team is the most successful national team in the world. They've won four World Cups and gold in four Olympic Games. They've never finished below third place in a World Cup. No other country comes close. So why are they so good?

## A Change in the Law

In 1972, a law called Title IX was passed in the USA. It meant that schools and universities had to treat sport for girls the same as for boys. Before this, girls' sports had often been ignored, but now they had to be taken seriously. More money and facilities meant that more girls started to play sport, and football was one of the most popular choices.

More girls in the USA were playing football than in any other country in the world. Because many other countries didn't want women playing football, the USA was at a huge advantage. Lots of players made it easier to find footballers with the talent to become the very best. That's exactly how it turned out for the US team.

## Inspiring Victories

The huge success of the US Women's National Team has inspired even more girls to take up the sport. The 1999 World Cup final against China was a great moment in US women's football. The 2019 US squad were children back then, and several of them took inspiration from watching the national side lift the cup. Christen Press, Megan Rapinoe and Alex Morgan have all said that watching the 99ers win made them realize that they wanted to do the same one day.

# France and Beyond

The US team dominated the 2019 World Cup in France, winning every match they played. On 7 July, they beat the Netherlands 2-0 in the final in front of a crowd of 58,000 people. There's no doubt this incredible team will have inspired another generation of girls to get out there and start kicking a ball about.

The rest of the world is slowly catching up to Team USA. Countries such as Sweden, Germany, Japan, England and Brazil are playing some brilliant football. It's a great thing for the sport – excellent teams spur each other on. Still, the US Women's National Team is likely to remain at the top of the game for years to come.

## FOOTIE FACT

In 1972, there were only 700 girls playing football at high school in the whole of the USA. By 1991 – the year of the first Women's World Cup – there were nearly 122,000. That's an increase of 17,000 per cent!

# MEGAN RAPINOE

**POSITION: FORWARD    COUNTRY: USA**

## EARLY YEARS:

Megan's older brother introduced Megan and her twin sister, Rachael, to football when they were just four years old. Both girls went on to play for teams coached by their dad. In high school, Megan and Rachael played for a women's team that was based two and half hours away from their hometown.

## ACHIEVEMENTS:

★ First player – male or female – to score a goal directly from a corner (known as an "Olimpico") at the Olympic Games.

★ Known for her inventive play and enthusiasm.

★ Won the Golden Ball AND Golden Boot at the 2⬤ Women's World Cup in France. FIFA named her ⬤ best women's player in the world in the same ye⬤

# ALEX MORGAN

"Always work hard, never give up, and fight until the end because it's never really over until the whistle blows."

**COUNTRY: USA**

**POSITION: FORWARD**

## EARLY YEARS:

Alex played lots of different sports as a child, but she started to take football seriously when she was 14. Right away, people noticed that she was something special. She was nicknamed "Baby Horse" because of her long, galloping strides.

## ACHIEVEMENTS:

★ The youngest US player at the 2011 Women's World Cup aged 22. Scored in both the semi-final and the final.

★ Won the Silver Boot at the 2019 Women's World Cup after scoring six goals.

★ Has scored more than 100 international goals, making her one of the leading scorers in US women's football.

★ Always pushes herself to the limit. Her runs off the ball are incredible.

# INSPIRING STORIES

## NADIA NADIM

Nadia grew up in Afghanistan, where football was banned by the Taliban, the political and religious group in charge of the country who imposed strict laws and restricted women's rights. Nadia's extraordinary story is one of tragedy and triumph.

## Playing in Secret

Girls weren't allowed to play any sport or even go to school under Taliban rule in Afghanistan, but Nadia was introduced to football by her dad. She had to kick the ball around in secret. Sadly, Nadia's dad was killed by the Taliban when she was 12 years old. Nadia fled the country with her mum and four sisters – it was too dangerous for them to stay.

The family landed in a refugee camp in Denmark. In the camp, Nadia played football with other kids from all over the world, and fell in love with the sport. It turned out that she was REALLY good at it.

## A Star in the Making

At club level, Nadia has played in Denmark, the USA, England and France. She's known for her energy and determination, and she's also brilliant at taking penalties.

Nadia started playing for local football clubs, and was soon spotted by the Danish national youth squad, who recognized her talent as a natural goal-scorer. FIFA made an exception and allowed her to play for the senior squad even though she hadn't been a resident in Denmark long enough for the official rules. She made her debut for the Danish team in 2009.

## More than a Footballer

Nadia uses her status to promote sport, education and equality. In 2019, she was named a UNESCO Champion for Girls and Women's Education. She speaks an amazing NINE languages and in 2022 she completed a medical degree, managing to juggle studying with a professional football career. She plans to become a reconstructive surgeon, giving people who've been injured a better future, when she retires from football.

"I hope that at the end of my career, I have shown some people that anything is possible. It doesn't matter where you come from or what you've been through. It just takes hard work and a belief in yourself and dreams do come true."

# GORGEOUS GOALS

There have been so many incredible goals in the women's game – almost too many to count! Here are a few of the most unforgettable of all time.

## CARLI LLOYD

### USA

#### USA v Japan, 2015 World Cup final

In a bold move, Carli Lloyd struck the ball from the halfway line. The Japanese keeper scrambled backwards, even getting a hand to the ball. But the ball hit the post and bounced into the back of the net, completing a hat-trick for Carli inside 16 minutes!

## BARBARA LATORRE

### BARCELONA

#### Barcelona v Espanyol, 2016

Barbara Latorre skilfully weaved through several defenders then was badly fouled. But she sprang back to her feet and managed to curl the ball past the goalkeeper to score against the team she used to play for.

## MARIE HAMMARSTROM

### SWEDEN

Sweden v France,
Third place play-off, 2011 World Cup

Following a corner, Marie Hammarstrom collected the ball outside the penalty area and flipped it right over the head of a defender. She beat another defender before striking the ball HARD into the back of the net. This gorgeous goal won the match – and third place in the World Cup – for Sweden.

## MARTA

### SANTOS

Santos v Juventus, 2011

Marta won the ball on the left wing, beat four defenders AND the keeper, then tapped the ball into the empty net with an audacious move known as a rabona. She had scored a goal with her legs crossed! Showing off? Probably. Very cool? Definitely.

# GREATEST OF ALL TIME

Marta Vieira da Silva is the greatest women's player of all time. She's changed the way people think about women's football.

## Brazilian Hero

Marta made her debut for the Brazilian national team in 2003. Since then she has been named FIFA World Player of the Year SIX TIMES, and in 2019 she became the first player – male or female – to score in FIVE World Cups. She also became the leading World Cup goal scorer of all time.

## A Difficult Start

Marta was better at football than some of the boys she played with in her hometown of Dois Riachos, Brazil. She was the only girl in a boys' football league, and many of the boys resented her. She had to play in football boots that were three sizes too big because there weren't any boots for girls – she stuffed paper in the toes to make them fit better.

In 2000, when she was 14, Marta moved to a town on the other side of the country to play for a women's team, but the club shut down. Many people in Brazil still held the old-fashioned view that women shouldn't play football. There just weren't enough opportunities for a player like Marta in her home country. She had to move abroad.

Marta moved first to Sweden, and then to the USA. She came back to Brazil for brief spells to play for the Santos women's team. But wherever she played, Marta dazzled with her talent.

Marta

# What makes Marta so good?

Marta has UNBELIEVABLE skills – her flair and creativity with a football are second to none. When she gets the ball at her feet, the other team had better watch out. She can dribble past defenders before they even know what's happening. Marta's passion for the game shines through, and her will to win means she never ever gives up. She always keeps her eyes on the prize: scoring goals, and lots of them!

When Brazil were knocked out of the 2019 World Cup, Marta made an emotional, inspiring speech addressed to young girls in Brazil:

"It's wanting more. It's training more. It's taking care of yourself more. It's being ready to play ninety plus thirty minutes. This is what I ask of the girls . . . The women's game depends on you to survive."

# INSPIRING STORIES

## LET US PLAY!

Around the world, girls are often stopped from playing on boys' football teams – even when there are no girls' teams for them to join. Some people are fighting back.

## Keep Playing

Seven-year-old Candelaria Cabrera from Chabás, Argentina, was the only girl playing in a children's football league. The football authorities said that Candelaria would have to play on a girls' team when she turned eight. But there wasn't a girls' team where Candelaria lived. When her mum, Rosana, broke the news to her, she was devastated.

Rosana started a campaign on social media. Members of the Argentinian women's national team got in touch to share the struggles they'd had, and to tell Candelaria they were behind her.

### Rosana's campaign worked!

The football authorities agreed that Candelaria – and other girls like her – could keep playing on mixed teams until the age of 11 rather than eight. They also created a football league for girls to join from the age of 12.

The first thing Candelaria did when she heard the news was convince her six-year-old sister to start playing football!

# Beating the Boys

The Spanish football club AEM Lleida decided to enter their Under-14s girls' team in an all-boys' football league. Some of the girls' parents thought it was a terrible idea – surely the girls would end up being humiliated?

At first the team suffered several defeats. They finished the season twelfth out of 18 teams. The players also had to put up with stupid comments from some spectators, and even referees. One referee insisted on calling the team "las princesas" (the princesses), which made the players angry.

In games and training, the AEM Lleida players focused on keeping possession – the other teams couldn't score goals if they couldn't get hold of the ball! The team's talent and hard work paid off. In 2017, AEM Lleida won the championship with just one defeat in the whole season.

One of the boys whose team was beaten said:

## "It's hard to lose against girls. But these ones really are very good."

Too true!

The team's incredible success led to more girls wanting to join the club. AEM Lleida now has EIGHT girls' teams. How brilliant is that?!

# FIGHT FOR WHAT'S RIGHT

Female footballers often have to fight to play the game they love. But they've had to fight hard for other things too.

## Fight to Choose

The hijab is a head covering worn by some Muslim girls and women. In 2007, FIFA decided that girls and women were not allowed to wear hijabs while playing football. FIFA said it was for safety reasons, even though there was no proof to back this up. The ban affected women and girls at all levels of the game. They were suddenly forced to choose between their religion and the game they loved.

There was a horrible incident in 2011. Players in Iran's national women's team were left crying on the pitch after a FIFA official refused to let them play in a match against Jordan to qualify for the Olympics because they were wearing hijabs.

Footballers and supporters – male and female – from all over the world came together to fight for the right of Muslim players to wear the hijab. Sportswear companies helped by designing hijabs that FIFA couldn't possibly have an issue with. The campaign was successful, and FIFA overturned their ban in 2014. Thank goodness they finally saw sense.

# Fight for Fairness

Female footballers earn far less money than male footballers – often less than a hundredth of the amount that men are paid for doing exactly the same job. It's not about money, it's about fairness. And many of the top players are sick of it.

In 2022, the US Women's National Team won a long legal battle to be treated the same as the men's team.

Megan Rapinoe said:

"We very much believe it is our responsibility, not only for our team and for future US players, but for players around the world."

From 2017 to 2022, Norway's Ada Hegerberg did not play for her national team as a protest against unequal treatment.

## FOOTIE FACT

In 2019, the Australian women's team made a deal to be paid the same as the men's team. Let's hope this is a sign of things to come around the world.

Ada said her protest had nothing to do with money, but with providing girls and women the same opportunities as men.

# FOOTBALL IS FOR EVERYONE

I think we can all agree by now that football is the best game on the planet. So the more people who can enjoy it, the better!

## Carson Pickett

Carson Pickett is one of the best defenders in the US National Women's Soccer League. She was born without a left forearm, and is one of the very few people with a disability at the top of any professional sport, though Carson uses the word "uniqueness" instead of "disability". She's exceptionally skilled at positional play – she thinks ahead so that she doesn't need to have a physical tussle for the ball.

In 2019, a toddler was in the crowd at one of Carson's matches. He was also born without a left forearm, and he was able to meet a top sportsperson who was just like him for the first time. It's totally brilliant for kids everywhere to see Carson Pickett excel at the very top level.

# Blind Football

Football for people with vision loss has been around for a while, but the women's game lags behind the men's. At the moment, the blind football tournaments at the Paralympic Games are only for men.

The women's game is playing catch-up. In 2017 and 2019 there were small training camps and tournaments held in Austria and Japan, and the first ever official women's World Championships took place in 2023.

There are different levels of vision loss, so all players except the goalkeeper wear eyeshades to make sure the game is fair. The goalkeeper is the only team member who is fully sighted. The ball is adapted to make a rattling or jingling noise so that players can hear where it is. Spectators have to be quiet to make sure players can hear the ball and each other.

It goes to show that, with a little thought and imagination, football truly can be for everyone.

# DID YOU KNOW?

Ali Krieger and Ashlyn Harris aren't just teammates on the US Women's National Team – they're teammates in life too, after getting married in 2019!

There are usually about half as many yellow cards in a Women's World Cup match as there are in a men's match. You can decide for yourself what that means . . .

Stephanie Frappart was the first woman to referee a major men's European match when she refereed Liverpool v Chelsea on 14 August 2019.

Norway's Caroline Graham Hansen scored the earliest penalty in a Women's World Cup when she put the ball in the back of the net against South Korea after just four minutes and 33 seconds.

Ecuador's Angie Ponce holds the record for the most own goals scored in a World Cup match (two), when she had terrible luck against Switzerland in 2015 . . . but she went on to score a penalty in the same game, Ecuador's first ever World Cup goal. What an emotional roller coaster!

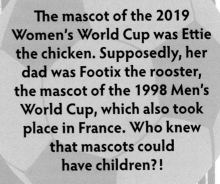

The mascot of the 2019 Women's World Cup was Ettie the chicken. Supposedly, her dad was Footix the rooster, the mascot of the 1998 Men's World Cup, which also took place in France. Who knew that mascots could have children?!

Denmark's Eggers Nielsen holds the record for the longest gap between World Cup goals. She scored in the 1995 World Cup and didn't score again until the 2007 tournament. A gap of 12 years and 98 days!

The Portland Thorns in the US National Women's Soccer League have dedicated fans. Their fan club, the Rose City Riveters, sing and chant NON-STOP throughout the games. There's even a list of the chants and songs on their website so you can learn them yourself.

# THE FUTURE'S BRIGHT

There's no doubt the journey of women's football has been a long one, and a tough one at times. But each generation has paved the way for the next, inspiring them to push harder. The game has never been in better shape than it is right now, and, with a little luck, things will just keep getting better and better.

## Rising Stars

Here are just a few of the amazingly talented footballers we can look forward to watching for years to come . . .

### Gift Monday
Nigeria

This powerful forward is always a threat in the air. She made her debut for the senior team in 2019 and is already making a big impact.

### Mary Fowler
Australia

The forward was just 16 when she travelled to France with the 2019 World Cup squad. She didn't get a chance to play, but she will certainly play a big role in Australia's future matches.

## Lena Oberdorf
### Germany

Aged 17 in the 2019 World Cup, she became the youngest player to represent Germany. She reached the final of EURO 2022 and was named the Young Player of the Tournament.

## Clàudia Pina
### Spain

She's scored LOTS of goals for Spain at youth level and is expected to do the same for the senior team. She's known for her eye for goal-scoring opportunities.

# Getting Started

Maybe you'd like to get out there and get playing, too. Maybe one day it will be YOU scoring a goal in a World Cup final, listening to the crowd roaring your name. How cool would that be? All you need to get started on that journey is a ball. And if you don't have a ball, you can scrunch up a piece of paper and use that in the meantime.

Or perhaps you prefer just watching football. There's never been a more exciting time to be a fan. Think of all the amazing goals, matches and tournaments to come. I for one can't wait!

## THE FUTURE IS BRIGHT.
## THE FUTURE IS FOOTBALL.

# INDEX

# CREDITS

The publisher would like to thank the International Olympic Committee for their kind permission to reproduce the Olympic Rings on pages 40 and 41.

The publisher would also like to thank the following for their kind permission to reproduce their photographs:

(Abbreviations key: t-top, b-bottom, r-right, l-left, c-centre, a-above, f-far)

**10** Everett Collection / Shutterstock (br); **11** Hulton Archive / Staff / Getty Images (tr); **12** Every effort has been made to trace the copyright holder and obtain permission to reproduce this image, please get in touch with any information relating to this image or the rights holder (tr); **14** Mirrorpix / Contributor / Getty Images (bl); **16** Bob Thomas / Contributor / Getty Images (lc); **25** Christof Koepsel / Staff / Getty Images (bc); **27** Laurence Griffiths / Staff / Getty Images (bl); **31** Andrew Katsampes/ISI Photos / Contributor / Getty Images (cr); **34** Pedro Vilela / Stringer / Getty Images (br); **36** Xinhua / Alamy Stock Photo (br); **41** Xinhua / Alamy Stock Photo (c); **43** dpa Picture-Alliance / Alamy Stock Photo (c); **50** Quality Sport Images / Contributor / Getty Images (b); **52** Natacha Pisarenko/AP / Shutterstock (b); **53** reproduced with kind permission of AEM Lleida (b); **54** Christopher Lee – FIFA / Contributor / Getty Images (b); **56** Icon Sportswire / Contributor / Getty Images (br); **61** Sirtravelalot / Shutterstock.